http://chef7star.webs.com/   Chef 7 Star

Other books by Chef 7 Star

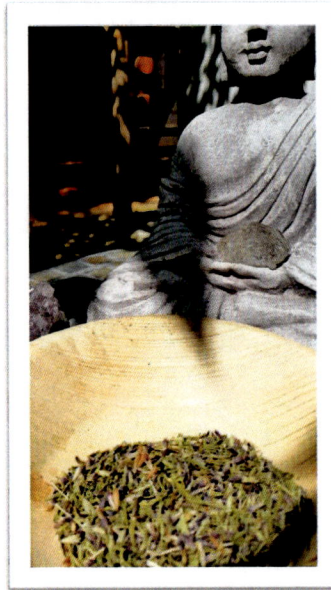

"The body and mind creates our temple . Place the gifts of nature's love and peace into your temple, and the temple will give long life and wellness to you."

Chef 7 Star

It helps to show photos of the possibilities of a living foods lifestyle ....
Once you become familiar with the recipes in this book, you will be able to create your own genre of RAW Vegan foods.

Enjoy this 10 page RAW Vegan food picture gallery with recipes in the following section!

Photos by Chef 7*

Chopped zucchini, tomato, olives and basil.

Carrot pate in flax almond bread with cashew cheese

Yellow squash pasta with slices of yellow squash and marinara covered squash and avocado slices

Zucchini "chicken" over cauliflower rice with oriental dressing

Italian herb dressed salad

Zucchini "drum" sticks

Stuffed zucchini blossom

Carrot pate and salad plates

SUNDRIED TOMATO AND SUNFLOWER
SEED CHILLI "BALLS" CAULIFLOWER
"RICE WITH SLICED ZUCCHINI

Zucchini pasta cashew Alfredo

Sunflower seed taco "meat" with cucumber "chips"

Coconut Curry dill dressing with mixed
green SALAD

"Batter" covered tomatoes

Fruit

Walnut coconut chocolate chip cookies

Zucchini spaghetti

Broccoli and yellow squash

Carrot, cucumber, pepper salad with
oriental ginger dressing

Sunflower seed and sundried tomato balls covered in "chili sauce" over cauliflower rice with spinach and cucumbers.

Chocolate crème filled walnut cake.

Southwestern seasoned sunflower seed, carrot, pepper balls.

Carrot pate sandwich

Cauliflower stuffed pepper

Oriental veggies

Middle eastern spiced cauliflower

salad

Nut cinnamon buns

<u>I don't get into actual knife sizes and stuff in this book but remember :</u>

Small slices of veggies makes for easier chewing when referring to salad creations.

A sharp knife is better than a dull knife. Invest in a knife sharpening stone.

Small knifes work best for creating thin slices.

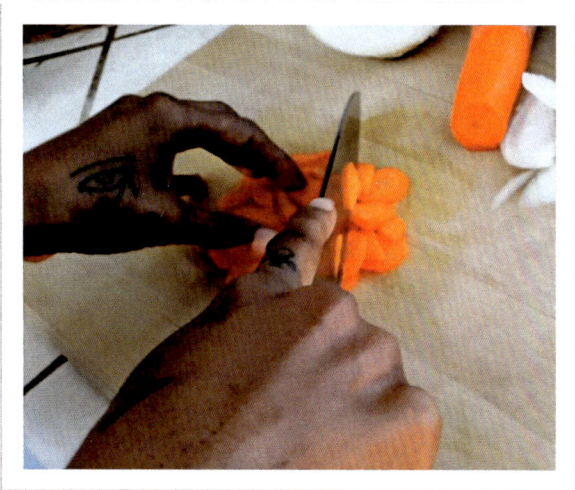

Photos of possibilities of a living foods ....

Photos by Cherf 7*

Party time finger foods with zucchini, sunflower seed, almond and flax seed crust pizza..

Next page Pizza as described in the sentence above, carrot pate with seaweed, curry spinach salad and seasoned green tomatoes.

Spinach avocado curry lemon salad

Seed pizza

Carrot pate with marinated collards & peas

Seed battered green tomatoes

Dehydrated broccoli

Marinara stuffed zucchini

Nut cinnamon sticky buns

Spicy BBQ cucumber chips

Walnut cinnamon vanilla mini cakes

Hummus burger

Zucchini strips

Garden eats!

Spicy salad with flax seeds

Coconut dill curry squash and green salad

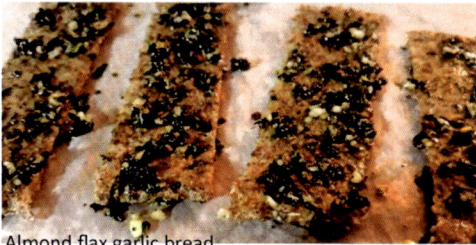

Almond flax garlic bread

Beets over spinach

Broccoli pasta

oranges

Salad Helper by Chef 7 Star ★

All natural ingredients

Great source of protein

Super delicious

Clean greens & sprinkle

Eating salads just got a whoooole lot easier!

I transitioned from the "standard American diet" into a healthier way of eating; if I can change my eating habits anyone can!

RAW foods are fresh un-cooked fruits, veggies, nuts and seeds.

I am inspired to create hearty, satisfying, cheesy, chewy, comforting goodness, using only RAW foods. Like most people I love FOOD that is *flavor-filled*, warm, chewy, cheesy, or crunchy.

My quest is changing the face of "salads" and I aim to change the approach to "healthy" eating to just eating tasty food!

Remember to pick up this book and stay away from the junk food!

I thank my husband, Artis E Hinson, founder of Body Ecology Life Sciences Attunement center and author of "From Dogma to Light", for introducing me to RAW foods; he is one of the pioneers of raw foods education and ancient essential oil therapeutics here in America.

I aspire to continue "wowing" the minds of all with my RAW food creations, beautifully crafted recipe books and inspirational life guide books!

Enjoy! ... and Thank you for your support!

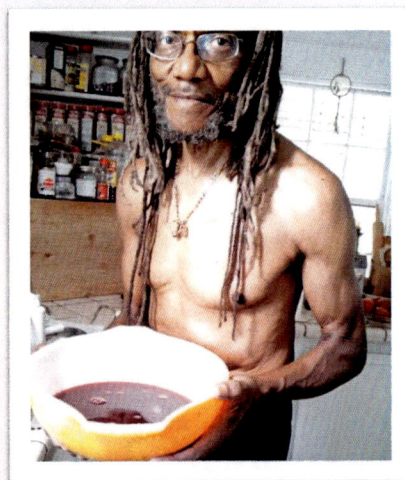

My husband Artis @ 71 years young

Bodyecol.webs.com

Keys to wellness with live foods:

1. Balance plant fibers with fruit acid. The fruit acid helps break down the plant fibers and the plant fibers help sweep the colon clean.

2. Cleanse the body with systems such as the "Ultimate Cleanse" in conjunction with more living foods.

3. Drink structured water for best results when cleansing and living a healthier life. (www.bodyecol.net for more info)

4. Carry snacks with you everywhere to prevent consuming things you don't "really" want.

5. Prepare goodies at your leisure to ensure you always have something good to eat.

6. Movement is vital to wellness. "Get up and jam to your favorite song."

7. Don't be too hard on yourself with concepts such as food combinations and certain "off" limit raw foods, at the beginning of your wellness journey. As you grow in wellness your mind and body will awaken to what you need for balance. In addition to this RAW comfort food; no rules apply, but that it be a fruit, veggie, nut or seed...oh and delicious!

8. Join pot lucks and congregate with others on a similar wellness path.

9. Enjoy time in nature. Align to the beauty of life within and without.

Why living/RAW foods?

We innately know that we should eat more fresh fruits and veggies. We all feel better when we are healthier. The detoxed, hydrated body is a health creating system. Living/RAW foods are fresh fruits, vegetables, nuts and seeds uncooked.

What are the benefits of eating raw?

I have more energy, creative ability, mental clarity, consistent weight and inner-peace since consuming only fresh fruits, vegetables, nuts and seeds. Read my mini book; 7 Steps to eat more living foods, for more eat RAW vegan food tips.

Is it easy to eat raw foods and cleanse?

It has not been an easy process to cleanse and re-program my mind and body. The difficulty was re-programing those cravings without giving in to them. I also learned to have patience with the process of detoxification, which can sometimes be uncomfortable. Staying on track with eating more RAW foods, makes each day following easier.

Let's prepare the kitchen

· Blender
· Mandolin(photo right)
· Dehydrator (Wooden dehydrator artslivejoybox.webs.com)
· Sharpe knives with knife sharpener
· Large stirring spoons
· Large mixing bowls
· "cheese" cutter (hand held slicer)
· Spiralizer (can find on amazon.com by name)

Let's get to the spices and things!

· Sea Salt
· Dry Basil
· Cayenne
· Garlic Powder
· Onion Power
· Crushed red peppers
· Organic Tamari (an aged soy sauce)
· Dried tomatoes
· Raw cashews
· Raw sunflower seeds
· Raw almonds
· If you like Garlic, always keep a bag of Garlic. Garlic makes everything taste better!
· Apple Cider Vinegar
· Olive oil(I prefer the non-cold pressed olive oil, because it is less bitter)
· For sweet a choice honey or agave nectar

Safety tips and other pointers

- Stay focused in the kitchen to prevent injury.

- When holding and cutting veggies always hold vegetables firm.

- Use a sharp knife to prevent injury when slicing fruits and vegetables (a dull knife will cut you quicker than it will a tomato).

- If someone walks in the kitchen while you are cutting, stop cutting to prevent injury.

- When using a food processor, remove blade before sticking fingers inside processor to remove food items.

- Soak all nuts and seeds before using. Soaked nuts are easier on the blender and on your digestive system. Soak all sunflower seeds, cashews, and almonds at least 6 hours.

- Always be mindful of salt, and sweetener, for excess of either will destroy any dish.

- Mince (small knife cuts) garlic and onion when adding pieces to salads and dressings (large pieces of garlic are a bit intense on the palate).

- Clean all veggies before use.

- Clean your hands well before preparing foods.

- Maintain joyful vibes when preparing foods.

What will be learned from this book?

- Nature's way of satisfying your cheesy, chewy, warm comfort food cravings!

- How to mix and match recipes to create a wide variety of wonderful comfort raw vegan meal creations.

- You will learn to face RAW food creation with confidence and clarity as you use your connection with the flavors, sights, and feels of these foods to cater to your unique desire. For example; add more spice, or more water; make your pizza dough thicker or thinner. I didn't write this recipe book for robots sooo.. use your imagination and techniques in this book to become your RAW vegan chef!

- If a recipe speaks of an item, please know the recipes embedded in recipes are found in this book.

- I do not provide exact measurements for recipes, it will be up to you to decide to add more or less of any ingredient to create the meal you desire. This book will share with you techniques, but it will be up to you to add the "magic" ingredient to bring these recipes to life.

- I designed this book to be inspiration. Be inspired and create living foods to nourish your body and feed your taste buds!

Sauces/Jelly

Section1

This section will cover the recipes for

- · "cheese"

- · Crème/frosting

- · Marinara

- · Jelly

- · Oriental dressing/ this stuff goes great on everything

- · Hot sauce/ sweet and sour sauce/ buffalo sauce

- * BBQ sauce

"Cheese"

"Cheese" is great for sandwiches, dipping, sauces, pizza and even more!

1 cup soaked cashews (soak cashews for about 6 hours)

½ cup water (Generally 1 cup nuts/seeds to ½ cup water)

1 1/ 2teaspoon sea salt

1/2 tablespoon garlic

½ tablespoon onion powder

1 tablespoon honey

1 lemon squeezed without seeds (use liquid only)

Blend ingredients until smooth (about 3 to 4 minutes)

This will make 1 cup of "cheese". This "cheese" will last about 1 week.

Crème

This crème also works well as a yogurt and whipped crème.

1 cup soaked cashews (6 hours)

½ cup of water.

Agave nectar (I prefer agave in sweet desserts) about 2 tablespoons and add vanilla according to taste

Blend ingredients until smooth (about 3 to 4 minutes)

This will make about 1 cup of crème.

Chocolate cacao sauce

1 tablespoons of cacao powder, ¼ teaspoon of coconut oil, 3 tablespoons of agave nectar. Blend in a bowl until smooth, with a fork or spoon. Use over ice cream or for any chocolate sauced goodies.

Marinara

Perfect for pizza sauce, chili, spaghetti, lasagna, pasta's and more. Add following ingredients together.

1/2 cup sundried tomatoes

1 and 1/2 large fresh tomatoes chopped

8 cherry tomatoes

2 cloves of minced garlic

1 tablespoon of chopped onion

Add water if blender slows down small amount at a time

1 tablespoon of honey

½ teaspoon of salt (add more or less)

Juice of 2 lemons

Blend until smooth (about 3-4 minutes)

Makes about 2 cups marinara. This will last for about 1 week.

Hot sauce

Use 2 tablespoons of marinara sauce

Add 1 teaspoon of sea salt

1 tablespoon of crushed red pepper (this is spicy, so use as you prefer)

¼ of a minced jalapeño

2 tablespoon of honey

2 cloves of minced garlic

1 teaspoon of minced onion

½ cup of apple cider vinegar

Combine all ingredients in a blender and blend for about 2 to 3 minutes. Add more marinara if sauce is too thin.

Oriental Sauce/Dressing

3 tablespoons of tamari

1/4 teaspoon of sea salt

6 tablespoons of olive oil

2 tablespoons of honey

Pinch of cayenne (if you dare)

½ tablespoon crushed red pepper

3 pieces of minced garlic

Stir in a bowl with a spoon

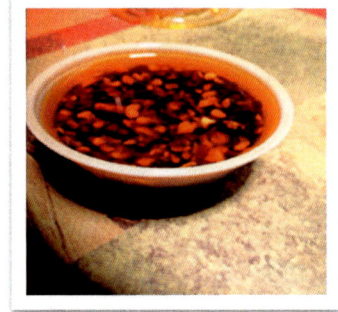

Chilli Sauce

Now we are going to make a chillisauce.

In a blender combine all following ingredients:

1/4 cup sundried tomatoes
2 dried chilies
1 tablespoon of red pepper flakes (spicy)
2 tablespoons of honey
1 teaspoon of sea salt
1 tablespoon chili powder
2 cloves garlic
1 slice of jalapeño about 1 teaspoon (if you want spice)
1 cup olive oil
Blend ingredients until smooth and add more water until you have a sauce consistency.

BBQ SAUCE

ADD TO A BLENDER:

1/2 cup apple cider vinegar	2 cloves garlic	1 tablespoon chilli powder
3 tablespoon honey	2 teaspoons of sea salt	1 pinch of chipotle spice powder
1 tablespoon red pepper flakes	about 5 sundried tomatoes	

Section 1

Cherry Jam/jelly

1. 1 1/2 cup of dry cherries or blue berries

2. 1/2 cup of water

3. 2 tablespoons of honey

4. Blend until smooth

5. Makes about 1 cup of jelly

6. Keeps about 1-2 weeks

In this chapter will discover the key to creating simple bread. This bread will be perfect for sandwiches, pies, cakes, pizza and more.

BREAD

Section 2

Bread/dough recipe

1 cup soaked almonds (soaked for about 6 hours)

1 cup flax seed powder (set to the side)

Blend Almonds in a blender with ½ cup of water to 1 cup almond.

Blend almonds with water, sea salt (1 large pinch), and honey(1 teaspoon) in the blender until smooth.

In a separate bowl add flax powder a bit at a time, to the almond blended mixture with hands. The flax will soak up excess water from the almond mixture. The mixture will begin to thicken as the flax is added and the batter is manipulated by hand, in a circular motion. When dough is ready it will not stick to fingers. It takes about 5 minutes to get the dough right.

Now you are ready to start making lots of great dishes. This bread does not require much time to dry. Depending on the thickness of the bread dish, drying can be as quick as 30 minutes to 1 hour. A dehydrator is needed. As you sample the bread every 30 minutes while it is in the dehydrator, you will decide when the bread is to your liking. Wax paper is needed to keep bread from sticking, as it is spread and shaped in your desired dishes.

Make some bread and keep it on hand for sandwiches. This recipe makes about 12 pieces of thin bread. We will also use this recipe to create mac and cheese and other great foods!

In this chapter we will discover the art of non-meat, non-fried options with fresh fruits and vegetables. I will share a battering technique which will transform all living foods into crunchy goodness!

Non fried crunchiness

DEHYDRATING

BATTERING

Section 3

Dehydration

The key to proper dehydrating is cutting the proper size for veggies and fruits. Thinner slices will ensure even drying and less drying time.

Dehydration removes the liquid from fruits and vegetables without changing the cellular structure of the fruit or vegetable. Dehydration eliminates the need to bake or fry foods, by creating various textures of dried foods.

The dehydrator should not reach temperatures over 120 degrees. Anything over this will "cook" the food and ruin the whole purpose of "RAW" eating.

RAW foods provide the body with enzymes. Enzymes are used to process the foods we eat, cleanse the digestion track and provide the body with energy. Cooked foods, unable to be used by the cells, congest the body, which is the reason for weight gain and illness.

Dehydrating is a wonderful way to transform fruits and veggies into wonderful RAW/Living comfort food. I don't suggest eating them everyday, and when you do add plenty of fresh veggies to them for easier digestion.

My husband builds wonderful wooden dehydrators.

http://artslivejoybox.webs.com/

The batter for all things

This batter will go on all things that will be dehydrated.

Battered foods are crisp and super delicious!

In a blender combine the following dry ingredients

1 cup of dry raw sunflower seeds

½ cup flax seeds

1 tablespoon garlic powder

2 tablespoons onion power

1 ½ tablespoon nutritional yeast (can be purchased at local health stores or online)

1 tablespoon of sea salt (when dehydrating use less salt, as the flavor will intensify as the foods dehydrate longer) ¼ teaspoon of cayenne

1. Blend into a powder and place in a plastic bag or glass jar. Use as needed.

2. When using keep amount being used separate from amount not being used.

3. A marinade will allow the batter to adhere to the object being battered .

Zucchini strip salad

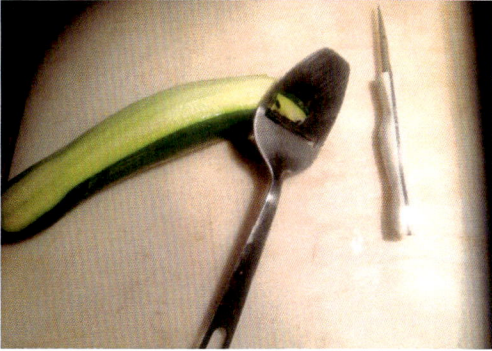

Step 1-2- removing skin and slicing.

Step 3-4- battering and dehydrating

Zucchini Strips

What you will need

A "cheese" cutter pictured previous page

1 large Zucchini

Batter from recipe in this book

1 large bowl

1. Use "cheese" cutter and peal the outer layer of the zucchini

2. Use the same "cheese" cutter, or knife and slice, long thin pieces of zucchini

3. Squeeze mixture of 1 lemon and 2 tablespoons of water over all sliced zucchini pieces.

4. In a dry bowl, place 1 cup batter and place zucchini in, 1 at a time covering each, front and back. Add more batter as needed. Place each battered zucchini on dehydration tray. Dry zucchini until crispy, which may be about 3-4 hours.

Add these awesome strip to your favorite salad for something special!

BBQ & MAC

BBQ

1. Prepare the zucchini strips recipe from previous recipe including the dehydration.

2. Apply bbq sauce (recipe in this book) on both sides of zucchini strip. Then place on wax paper and allow to dehydrate for about 1 hour.

   Then they are done! Enjoy with Mac and Cheese for a southern delight!

French Fries

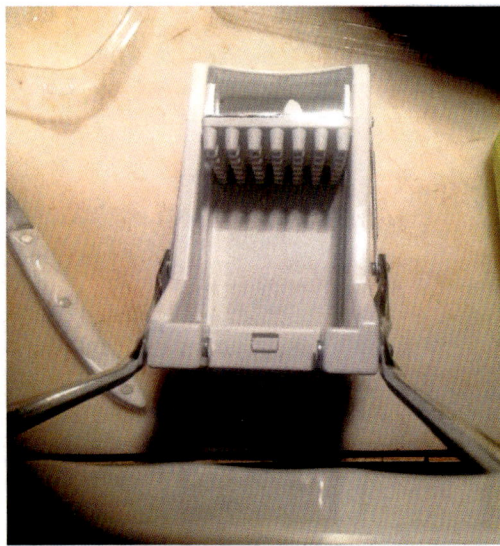

French Fries

1.   1 large zucchini

2.   Use a French fry cutter (which can be purchased online) or a knife and slice the cleaned zucchini into French fry sizes.

3.   Add fries to a bowl.

4.   Marinate the fries so that the batter made with 1 lemon, 1 teaspoon of garlic and 1 teaspoon onion powder, will adhere .

5.   In a separate bowl add 1 cup of dry batter from recipe In this book.

6.   Each fry will have to be covered by hand separately, so be patient and cover the entire French "frie" to ensure crunchiness. Add more batter as needed.

7.   Place each fry separately, onto the dehydration pan and allow fries to dry for about 3-5 hours, until crispy, yet not too hard. Taste a fry every hour to see how you prefer them.

8.   Use marinara recipe from this book as the "ketchup" and enjoy!

Zucchini wrap with fries

1. Use the zucchini strip recipe from this book. Take the end product and create your wrap.

2. Use a cleaned romaine leaf and place dehydrated zucchini strip inside with chopped lettuce, tomato, and your favorite vegetables. Add hot sauce recipe from this book and drizzle wrap with sauce.

3. Add French fries from the recipe in this book and enjoy.

Sun beam Tempura string beans

1. Soak cleaned string beans in oriental marinade recipe from this book for about 2-3 hours in the sunlight.

2. Next use the batter recipe from this book and batter each string bean until fully coated.

Serve and enjoy!

Sweet and Sour "Z"hicken

1. Peal zucchini removing green skin.

2. Carefully slice 1 inch squares .

3. Dip the pieces into a bath of water, 1 lemon, 1 teaspoon of olive oil and sea salt.

4. Next use the batter recipe from this book and batter the entire piece of zucchini. Repeat this entire batch. Dehydrate pieces for about 2 hours to allow batter to stick to zucchini

5. Next use the hot sauce recipe from this book and coat each piece of zucchini once it has dehydrated (step 4.)

6. Allow coated zucchini to dehydrate for about 2 hours and then enjoy!

7. To alternate into "sweet and sour" simple add more honey to hot sauce recipe

Buffalo Bites

In this section we will combine all things crème. I will demonstrate how we can transform one ingredient into various wonderful dishes.

All things Crème and jelly

Section 4

Ice Cream

1. Use the recipe for crème in this book add 2 tablespoons of coconut oil.

2. Freeze overnight or use ice cream maker, which can create ice cream in about 25 minutes.

3. This makes a perfect simple ice cream.

4. Top with cacao sauce recipe from this book, if you'd like.

Yummy!

CAKE

1. Use the bread recipe in this book adding 2 tablespoons of agave nectar to its dough. Once bread is mixed by hand, pat out layers into desired shape and size (the layers shouldn't be too thick).

2. Dehydrate cake layers for about 1 hour keeping the layer slightly moist and flexible.

3. Next layer the cake by placing cream below, between stacked bread pieces .

4. Prepare the crème recipe in this book, which makes about 1 cup and set to the side.

5. Cover all layers and the entire cake with crème, and set in the fridge for about 1 hour. Add strawberries or any other sweet topping.

Enjoy!

Breakfast is served, view next page for pancake recipe!

Pan Cakes and Jelly

1. Use the bread recipe from this book, shape the dough into mini circles

2. (Don't shape too thick) about 1/2 inch thick.

3. Dehydrate the mini circles for about 1½ hours; dehydrate up to 3 hours for firmer pancakes.

4. I like the pancakes dehydrated for less time, because they are chewy.

5. I want you to learn to make these recipes perfect for you.

6. Add "jelly" recipe or the strawberry sauce recipe, from the parfait page of this book to your pan cakes.

1. Use 1 cup of crème (recipe from this book). This is the yogurt part of the parfait.

2. In a blender combine 1 hand of cleaned strawberries, with 1 tablespoon of honey and the juice of 1 lemon. Blend for about 10 seconds.

3. For crumbles in a bowl, combine handful of raw dry walnuts with 1 teaspoon of agave nectar. With the hands, crumble these 2 ingredients together. This will make the "granola" part of the parfait.

4. Combine layers of walnut crumbles, strawberry sauce, and cashew crème in a cup.

5. Now you are ready!

Serves 1 ~Enjoy.

Chocolate Sunday

1. Use 1 cup of crème recipe from this book. This is the yogurt part of the parfait.

2. Add 1 tablespoon of cacao sauce recipe from this book, and blend with 1 cup of crème, to make chocolate Sunday.

3. For crumbles in a bowl combine 1 handful of raw dry walnuts, with 1 teaspoon of agave nectar or honey. Crumble these 2 ingredients together by hand.
This will make the "cookie" part of the Sunday.

4. In a cup, combine in layers walnut "cookie" crumbles, cacao sauce, and cashew crème. Set in the freezer for about 2 hours and enjoy!

Serves 1

Cinnamon Rolls

Cinnamon rolls

1. start with a ball of dough created from this book

2. Next gather a baseball size amount of dough and roll flat on wax paper about the thickness of a nickel

3. Spread dough with a mixture of 1 tablespoon cinnamon, 4 table spoons evaporated cane sugar (substitute cane sugar with honey spread evenly then sprinkled with cinnamon.)

4. Carefully roll the dough in to a roll

5. Then slice 1 inch pieces and place each in the dehydrator. Allow mixture to dehydrate for about 5 hours.

6. To make the frosting use the "crème" recipe from this book and spread evenly on top.

7. Place back in dehydrator for about 1 hour if you desire a warm dessert and enjoy when ready!

8. Chop some pecans and place them on top!

PB & J

For a wonderful snack!

1. Use the dehydrated bread (from recipe in this book) that you may have on hand.

2. Add jelly recipe from this book with almond butter (which can be purchased raw at local health food stores, or if you are familiar with raw foods you can make it yourself, wonderful demo videos online).

3. Combine like a regular peanut butter and jelly sandwich and enjoy!

Berry Pie

1. Use the simple jelly recipe and refrigerate overnight to thicken.

2. Use bread recipe and place ingredients into a pie pan.

3. Be sure to take your time and pat dough into pan evenly as you would regular pie dough.

4. Next add your jelly to the crust

5. Use left-over bread dough flattened on waxed paper. Cut into slices and top pie. Use photo as a model.

6. Dehydrate for about 1 hour. Slice and serve.

In this section we are going to combine all things "cheese" for wonderful cheesy creations!

ALL THINGS "CHEESE"!

Section 5

Pizza

1. Use the bread recipe from this book.

2. Shape the dough into a pizza size, about 1/4 inch thick.

3. Top the crust with marinara and the "cheese" (recipes in this book). It is best to make the "cheese" and "marinara" recipes (in this book) prior to making your pizza.

4. Always make enough sauces to have more than you need. Next, top the pizza with your favorite veggies and fruits.

5. Dehydrate the pizza for about 2 hours and enjoy!

Zandwhich

1. Use dehydrated bread recipe from this book and begin building your sandwich. Keep dehydrated bread on hand to make wonderful sandwiches at your desire.

2. Use dehydrated zucchini strip recipe from this book to top sandwich.

3. Use about 3 zucchini strips per sandwich and add toppings of lettuce, tomatoes, and a little "cheese" (recipe from this book) and enjoy.

Calzones

To create a calzone, Super raw comfort!

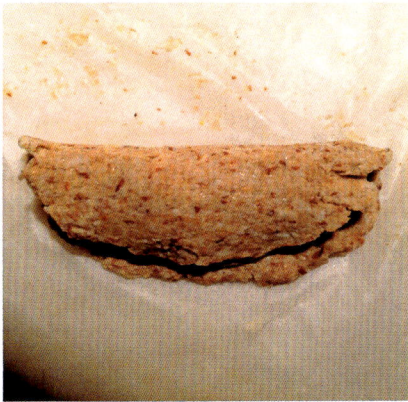

Step 1– create dough recipe from this book

Step 2– create the "cheese" recipe from this book

Step 3—take golf ball size ball of dough (maybe a bit more) and pat into a circle on wax paper with fingers. Try to achieve thickness of a nickel.

Step 4– Add the "cheese" along with any other ingredients of your choice.

Step 5– Close the calzone carefully and seal with a fork similar to the photo.

Step 6– place calzone in the dehydrator for about 3-4 hours

Use the marinara recipe from this book as a dip!

Enjoy

"Grilled Cheeze"

Use the dehydrated bread from the recipe in this book, then take finished dried pieces shaped as seen in photo.

1. Add "cheese" from recipe in this book to the bread

2. Place in the dehydrator for about 2 hours and enjoy!

Jalapeño Poppers

Jalapeño Poppers

What you will need:

1/2 cup "cheese" from the recipe in this book.

1/2 cup marinara from the recipe in this book.

Dough created from the recipe in this book

2 finely chopped jalapeño's

(if you are creating this recipe and it sticks to your hands add more flax to your batter.)

Use patience with good hand-eye coordination

1. Pull off about half of golf ball size of dough and shape in hand. Turn your hand into a fist with dough inside and close all ends so "cheese" does not slip out. Leave tunnel open at the top , this is where we will place cheese and jalapeño pieces.

2. Next in a bowl combine jalapeño with cheese (you may not need this entire batch) .

3. Fill the "popper" dough closed on all ends yet open in the top with the jalapeño/ cheese mixture and carefully align in a dish.

4. Once you have created as many poppers as you want , place the poppers into the dehydrator for about 2 to 4 hours, and enjoy with a side of marinara.

Quesadilla

Quesadilla

1. To prepare this simple treat use the same calzone recipe from this book Allow "cheese" filled calzone to dehydrate for about 3-4hours.

2. Next slice dehydrated calzone into 3 triangle quesadilla pieces.

3. In a separate bowl make your salsa. By combining 1 chopped tomato, 1 tablespoon of minced purple onion, juice of 1 lime, 1 tablespoon of minced cilantro, 1 clove of minced garlic, and 1/3 teaspoon of sea salt.

Serve as pictured above and enjoy!

Spinach Pie

Spinach Pie (makes 2 pies)

1. Use the dough from recipe in this book

2. Line the pie pan with dough about the thickness of a nickel

3. To make filling: combine 3 hands full of cleaned spinach with 1/3 cup of cheese from the recipe in this book. Stir ingredients together well!

4. Next flatten a golf ball sized amount of dough into a flat square of wax paper and with a knife, carefully slice pieces of dough into strips and place on top of your pie.

5. Dehydrate your pies for about 2-3 hours

6. Add some cherry tomatoes right before serving and enjoy!

Quiche

1. Use the bread recipe from this book to make your crust.

2. Line a glass or pie pan with "dough"

3. Add 1 cup of fresh spinach to a bowl with about 1/3 cup of "cheese" recipe from this book (to feed more people, use more of either ingredient as this recipe serves about 2). Blend ingredients spinach and cheese together with a large spoon. Add this mixture to the pan on top of the crust shaped in the dish .

4. Top pan with marinara sauce from this book.

5. Add tomato slices on top and spinach leaves.

6. Allow this dish to dehydrate for about 1-2 hours

Serve and enjoy!

Pot Pie

1. Use bread recipe from this book. Place dough into a pan at desired "pie crust" thickness about that of a nickel. Dehydrate the crust for about 30 minutes.

2. In a separate bowl combine ½ cup fresh peas , 3 tablespoons of minced carrots, and 1 1/2 tablespoons of minced onion.

3. Combine ½ cup of cashew "cheese" from recipe in this book with the veggies . Fill the crust with the cheesy"veggies.

4. Gather more dough and flatten onto wax paper. Cut extra dough into strips and place on top of your pie. Dehydrate for 1to 2 hours.

   Enjoy!

Mac and "Cheese"

Making Mac and "Cheese"

Step 1. Make dough recipe from this book and lace on wax paper.

Step 2. gather golf ball size of dough and rub in-between hands in a back and forth motion.

Step 3. Allow 1 inch pieces or desired size to fall away and continue rubbing until you have created the amount of noodles desirable.

Step 4. Dehydrate the pieces of noodles for about 1 hour to remove excess moister.

Step 5. In a large bowl stir in the cheese, created from the recipe in this book. Use as much as you desire.

Step 6. Dehydrate the mixture for about 1 hour and serve!

Ravioli

1. Use the dough recipe from this book

2. With a rolling pin, flatten out a 4 oz size dough ball, as thin as possible, on a counter or board, lined with wax paper.

3. Next use the 1/2 cup, of the "cheese" recipe from this book, combined with 3 hands full of cleaned & chopped spinach. Then stir until well blended and set this in a bowl.

4. Now cut your dough into 2 inch squares and thickness of a nickel. Place the spinach, cheese mixture inside. Be sure not to over stuff, as this will not allow the ravioli to close properly.

5. Next cut another square equal to the first and place carefully on top without mashing the middle. Then take a fork and close the ends of each ravioli.

6. Make as many as you wish and place in the dehydrator for about 2 hours.

7. Once the ravioli is done top with marinara from the recipe in this book. Use as much as you'd like.

Serve and enjoy!

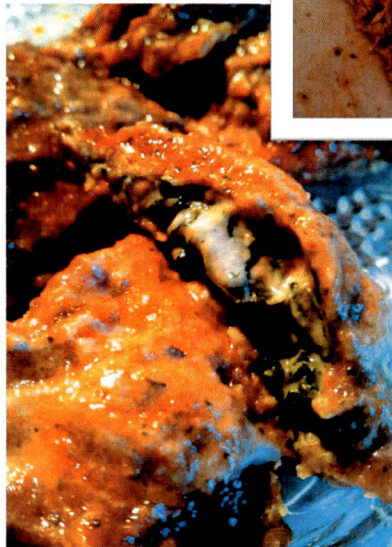

Mushroom Filled Ravioli

1.Use the same techniques described on the previous page to create the dough and start the ravioli.

2.In a bowl combine 1/2 cup of cheese to about 10 mushrooms. cleaned/ with brown stems removed. Place this mixture in the dehydrator for about 2 hours, to soften the mushrooms and remove excess water.

3. Now fill your ravioli with the mushroom mixture and dehydrate all pieces for about 2 to 4 hours.

4. When your ravioli has finished dehydrating before serving, add any left over cheese and mushrooms on top with any of your other favorite veggies.

Mushroom Pizza

To create you will need:

1/2 cup "cheese" recipe from this book.

Dough recipe from this book

1 cup thinly sliced and cleaned mushrooms

1/2 thinly spiced jalapeño

1. roll out your dough into less than 1/8 inche thick circle on wax paper (use as much dough as you'd like to make the pizza as big as you want it)

2. Spread the cheese on evenly

3. Add sliced mushrooms and jalapeño to the pizza

4. Sprinkle with a bit of basil and dehydrate for about 3 hours

5. Slice and enjoy.

Manicotti

Manicotti

To create this recipe you will need:

Dough created from recipe in this book

1/2 cup marinara recipe from this book

1/2 cup cheese

 4 hands full of spinach

1. combine cleaned spinach that has been finely chopped in a bowl with the 1/2 cup of "cheese" and stir well.

2. Next use your hand and press a golf boll sized piece of dough, into a circle about the thickness of a nickel.

3. In the center of that flatted dough place the spinach and cheese mixture.

4. Now roll the dough over the center filling and connect to the space outside the filling. Then roll the remaining piece over and close.

Kale Gyro

Kale Gyro

1. In a separate bowl place 1 bunch of cleaned and chopped kale. Be sure to remove stem, as it is hard to chew.

2. Add to same bowl, 1 cup of prepared "cheese" from the recipe in this book.

3. Next blend the kale and "cheese" together

4. Prepare the dough recipe from this recipe

5. Gather a golf ball sized amount of dough and pat with fingers on wax paper into a circle shape, about thickness of a nickel

6. Next add ingredients to the inside of the dough (photo above)

7. Then roll over and seal the end of the "gyro"

8. Place wrap in the dehydrator for about 1 hour and devour!

Chilli "Cheese" Fries

Chilli "Cheese" Fries

1. Create the chilli recipe from this book and set to the side.

2. Create French fry recipe from this book and dehydrate about 2-3 hour (as you prefer them)

3. Next create the "cheese" recipe from this book and place in a bowl aside.

4. On a plate place the French fries then top with chilli and then finish the dish with "cheese" and serve.

Oriental Flavors

Section 6

7 Star food photos

Oriental Noodles

7 Star food photos

In a bowl combine-

½ broccoli head

1 chopped carrot

1 table spoon of minced onion,

1.   Create noodles from 1 large Zucchini (use a veggie spiralizer, which can be found online and is a must have in the kitchen/ photo below). If you don't have a spiralizer, you can use a mandolin slicer .

2.   Combine ingredients in a bowl with desired amount of oriental sauce recipe from this book. Allow ingredients to marinate for about 2 hours. Don't stir just mix with hands. this will prevent zucchini noodles from breaking down. This recipe is the oriental noodles.

Oriental Noodle Wraps

1. Lay out flat piece of "nori" seaweed and add ingredients from previous recipe.

2. Use a small vassal of water to seal ends of seaweed only rolled. View next page for visuals.

3. Use a sharp knife to cut small pieces, once the salad is rolled in the nori.

Oriental noodle wraps

Oriental Carrot Noodles

Oriental Carrot Noodles

1. I love the manner that raw dishes can be switched up, creating a totally new dish.

2. Peel the outer layer of a large carrot. Use the spiralizer tool or a mandolin (can be found online) and create carrot noodles. You can even use shredded carrots.

3. 1 large carrot

4. ½ broccoli head (or more if you like)

5. 1 tablespoon minced onion

6. 1 hand full of minced purple cabbage

7. Add some dry seaweed if you like that flavor.

8. Combine all ingredients into a bowl. Pour your desired amount of oriental sauce over salad and serve.

Mushroom steak with salad

1. Use oriental sauce from this book and marinate 2 large cleaned and chopped Bella mushrooms (about 3 hours), until mushrooms absorb the marinade.

2. *Chop mushrooms into shapes like the photo above.

3. Marinate 2 bunches of cleaned spinach with oriental sauce until spinach wilts. Marinating is a wonderful way to enhance flavors and soften vegetable textures.

4. Add fresh heirloom tomato slices, chopped carrots and serve.

Oriental String Beans

1. Marinate cleaned string beans in oriental dressing from this book for about 2-3 hours in the hot sun or in the dehydrator for about 2-3 hours and serve.

Mr.Chow's Plate of oriental Veggies and Cauliflower Sticky Rice

Mr. Chow's

Tools needed

Cutting board

2 large bowls

Food Processor or sharp large knife

What you will need:

Serves 1-2

1/2 cauliflower diced

1/2 avocado

6 pieces of mushroom cleaned and sliced

1 zucchini sliced into disks 1/2 inch thick

1 carrot sliced as thin as you can

1/4 sweet onion sliced thinly

1 small crown of broccoli cleaned and cut into small pieces from stem to top leaving bushy top together.

Combine all ingredients except the cauliflower into a bowl and set aside.

What to do:

Create the Oriental dressing from page 12 in this book!

Set dressing aside to use later

Take your chopped veggies and add 1/2 of the made sauce to them and place in an air tight container, then sit under the sun for about 3-4 hours to allow them marinate.

To create "sticky rice" either chop 1/2 head of cauliflower small with large knife on a cutting board or place 1/2 cauliflower diced into a food processor and pulse about 4 times. (be sure to pulse too long or cauliflower will loose its texture.)

After your cauliflower is shredded add to a large bowl and peel the skin from your avocado and remove the seed and add inner green parts of the avocado to your "rice" and add 1 tablespoon of oriental dressing to it and use a large spoon to combine avocado into cauliflower until creamy and no chunks. Now taste, you may need to add a pinch of salt or more oriental dressing, the choice is yours.

Next remove veggies from sun marinating and squeeze off excess liquid then add to a plate on top of a serving of the cauliflower rice and pour more Oriental dressing on top.

Everything Marinara

Section 7

Zucchini Rolls filled with spinach and marinara

1. Clean zucchini and remove outer green layer with cheese cutter.

2. Lay out flat pieces of zucchini.

3. In a separate bowl, combine ½ cup of marinara with 1 bunch of cleaned, chopped spinach and stir together.

4. On each piece of zucchini add a spoon of marinara/spinach mixture.

5. Even add "cheese" recipe from this book, if you dare!

6. Sprinkle dry basil on the outside and enjoy.

Lasagna

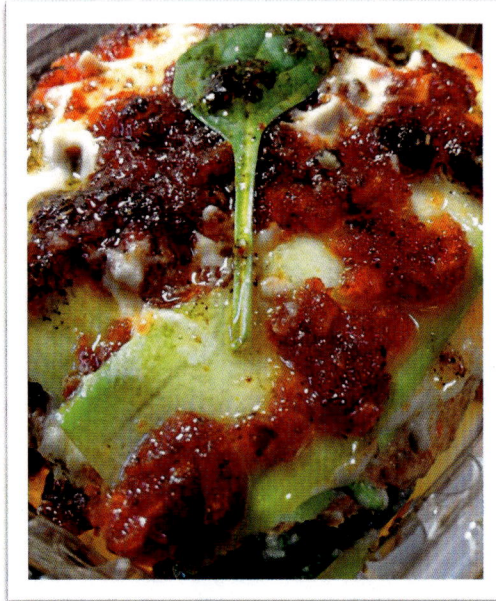

Lasagna

To make super <u>lasagna</u>, Create zucchini strips with a knife by slicing "lasagna" size noodles, using the peeled zucchini. I find a "cheese" slicer is much easier to create long, flat, "noodle" size pieces.

In a bowl, combine 1 bunch of cleaned, chopped spinach with ½ cup of "cheese", recipe from this book. Be sure that you have enough cheese to make as much lasagna as you'd like.

Build lasagna in a baking pan. Start by placing marinara on the bottom layer. Make the marinara recipe from this book to be sure that you have enough to spread around.

Next add the "cheese" and spinach mixture from the bowl.

Then place a layer of zucchini strips, top with more marinara and dehydrate for about 1 hour and serve.

Pasta

1. Take 1 large zucchini and peel outer skin

2. Use the "cheese" cutter and slice noodles into long 1/2 inch wide pieces, with a knife; As in photo above.

3. Blend noodles in a bowl with marinara recipe from this book (it's your choice to use a lot or a little) add 1 cup of chopped spinach.

4. Stir and serve.

Chilli

1. Prepare chilli sauce recipe from this book and set aside.
2. In a bowl add the following ingredients:
3. chop ½ celery
4. 1 chopped green pepper
5. 1 chopped red pepper
6. ¼ onion
7. 1 half cauliflower head
8. Add to the bowl of veggies the cihlli sauce and stir together.

Add a pinch more any additional spice to create your flavor kick.

Serve and enjoy!

Spaghetti!

1. Take 2 zucchini and peel outer layer with cheese cutter, removing the stem.
2. Create your zucchini noodles using a spiralizer or mandolin and sit to the side.
3. In a bowl combine ½ chopped green pepper
4. ¼ purple chopped onion
5. Add to this bowl 1 cup of marinara from recipe in this book.
6. Stir and add 1 teaspoon of dried basil to the sauce bowl mixture.
7. Once you place the zucchini noodles on the plate top with basil, green pepper and onion marinara sauce, next add black olives (remove the pits), chopped cucumber and sliced organic cherry tomatoes and sprinkle of black pepper to compete this spaghetti plate.

*Remember to be creative and add more sea salt if needed or any other ingredient you feel will make this recipe uniquely yours.

Extra Recipes

Garlic Cauliflower Mash!

Ingredients:

1/2 head of cauliflower

1/4 cup of "cheese" recipe from this book

Tools:

Food processor, stirring spoon and bowl

1. Add cauliflower that has been chopped small to processor. Be sure not to over power your processor, and process small batches at a time. To the processor add 1/4 cup "cheese" to cauliflower and process for about until smooth. Top with more cheese when done!

I sprinkle a bit of black pepper to mine! Enjoy!

Sun Seed Taco

Sun Flower Seed Taco

Ingredients:

1/2 cup soaked sunflower seeds

6 pitted olives chopped and minced

2 cloves minced garlic

1 teaspoon honey

1/2 lemon squeezed with out seeds

3 sun dried tomatoes chopped small

2 tablespoons chopped carrot

1 tablespoon chopped sweet onion

8-10 Romaine leafs

1 dozen cherry tomatoes diced

1 packet all natural taco seasoning

(all natural seasonings can be purchased from natural food stores.)

Tools:

- Food processor
- Or Sharpe knife and cutting board.
- Large spoon

Steps:

- 1st pour off soaking water from the soaked sunflower seeds. Soak sun-flower seeds for at least 5 hours.

- Next place soaked seeds in the food processor with 3 chopped sun dried tomatoes, 1 tablespoon of sweet onion, 1/2 lemon juice, 1 teaspoon honey, 2 cloves of minced garlic, 2 tablespoon of carrots chopped and 1/2 packet of natural taco seasoning (taste and add more once all ingredients are processed). Some packets have salt and sometimes they may not have salt added; read ingredients and add salt to taste if needed; be sure to add pinches until desired flavor.

- Next process ingredients until finely combined, yet with texture. Pulsing the processor works well to reach desired texture. Pulse at least 12x

- Now take your romaine leaf and add the taco "sun flower meat" and top with sliced cherry tomatoes and minced olives.

- For added flavor use "cheese" or "chilli sauce recipes from this book, for additional sauciness to top your romaine taco.

Other uses of Taco "sunflower seed meat " from previous recipe

Add to come veggies, atop some almond bread for a cultural dish.

Roll balls of the sunflower seed "meat" and stick a toothpick in them. Great party food!

More uses of Taco "sunflower seed meat " from previous recipe

Add sunflower seed "meat" atop some cucumbers, sprinkled with cayenne and black pepper, then top with jalapeño pieces for delicious "chip and dip" like eats.

Wrap sunflower seed "meat" in collard leaf

Okra Stuffed Tomatoes

What you will need:

1 cup of marinara from this book

10 thinly sliced, cleaned pieces of okra

1 large diced tomato

Salt and pepper for taste

1. In a large bowl combine okra and tomatoes with the marinara and stir well

2. Next slice half a large tomato and gut the insides with a spoon; add the inner tomato to the bowl with the okra and tomato and stir.

3. Use the cleaned tomato and fill each half with the okra mixture and serve! Enjoy

A NUTTY TREAT

Ingredients:

- 1 hand full of pecans
- 1 hand full of almonds
- 1 and of sunflower seeds
- 1 hand of raisons
- 1 hand of dried cranberries
- 1 hand of pumpkin seeds
- 1 hand of walnuts

Add all to food processor and process until every ingredient is blended well!

Once it is processed this treat is ready to eat. Add to muffin cups or a large pan and slice into squares and put up some for a healthy snack.

Tools:

- Food processor
- Hands

Walnut Chocolate muffins

Ingredients:

- 1/2 cup of walnuts
- 3 tablespoons of Hershey's cacao unsweetened
- 4 tablespoons of honey (add more if desired)
- 1 pinch of sea salt

Tools:

- Measuring utensils
- Cupcake pans and liners
- Food processor

1st step add all ingredients to the food processor and blend until it looks like a batter or dough.

Add more honey at this point, if you feel this dish needs it.

Then use a cup cake pan with liners and add batter to each cupcake mold.

Sit the pan with batter in it in the freezer until firm.

*If you blend ingredients properly in the processor without over processing, these cakes will be ready and won't need to be placed in the freezer to firm up!

Enjoy!

3 Day Detox

Use the recipes below and repeat for 3 days to detox with raw foods! These meals are meant to help with the transition into simpler foods. The recipes on this page and the following pages are simple and will support balance of fruits, veggies and nuts.

To help with digestion I recommend drinking lemonade (a combination of lemons, water and honey) at the beginning of the day, before bed and or as a snack along with this meal plan. Add about 8 lemons to 1 half gallon of water, sweeten with honey to taste.

Great grape Smoothie!

1st juice your fresh grapes (I love grape juice as the base for my smoothies)

Next add grape juice to blender about 2 cups

Add 1/2 of papaya including seeds minus the skin of the papaya to blender

Then add 2 chopped strawberries with the tops removed to blender

Remove 1/2 of avocado from it's shell (toss the shell) add to blender

Remove the skin from 1 banana and place in the blender

Now, blend all together until smooth. There you have it!

Italian Herb Salad dressing

½ cup of Italian Herb Blend (one can purchase this from an herb dealer or in the spice aisle of the market)

2 cups of olive oil (one can use either cold pressed or regular, I like the taste of regular olive oil better)

4 cloves of garlic

½ table spoon of sea salt

½ jalapeno

Honey to taste

Blend with blender and taste, add more or less of sweetener, spice or lemon for tang. Use this dressing, over everything mostly.

Divine Salad

Red leaf lettuce cleaned and separated, ½ small, chopped purple onion

2 carrots peeled and chopped into small pieces

Combine the above mixture in a plastic container; this is tasty for 4 days

* The flax and nori, should be added before serving

1 hand full of flax seeds sprinkled on top

2 pieces of nori seaweed paper chopped into small pieces

Combine into a bowl. I recommend using Italian Herb Dressing.

*Roll this salad in nori Seaweed Paper, sealing the ends with water; makes great finger foods when sliced into 3 inch pieces.

Now that you have the detox recipes, here is the plan

Start your day with 2 glasses of structured water

(for more info contact bodyecol. 336 273 7406).

Water can be structured through crystals and frequencies of energy.

Drink 1 glass of lemonade 1 hour after each meal of breakfast, lunch and dinner.

Breakfast: Slice 1 Orange and 1 mango or kiwi and eat

Breakfast should be lite to allow full energy to flow for the day.

Lunch: Great Grape smoothie

Smoothies are a great way to feel full without the heaviness.

Dinner: large divine salad with Italian herb dressing.

Keep in mind that as you grow in RAW foods preparation skills you can create many different snacks. My favorite snacks are kale chips, olives, lemonade, and fruit.

Any questions about detoxing just email me: illum7ination@yahoo.com

Established in 1975

Body Ecology Life Sciences Attunement Center, is dedicated to providing unique personalized service.
We ship products for your convenience.

We blend formulas for any condition based on your date of birth from natural herbs.

These products include but are not <u>limited to:</u>

-natural Weight off

-herbal detox #1 seller

-pain formula for arthritis

-natural tooth care

-personalized cologne

-books

- colloidal gold and copper

-astrological readings

-quality skin care

-herbs and more

- structured water

Husband wife owners/operators

336 273 7406   bodyecol.webs.com

Another recipe book by Chef 7 Star

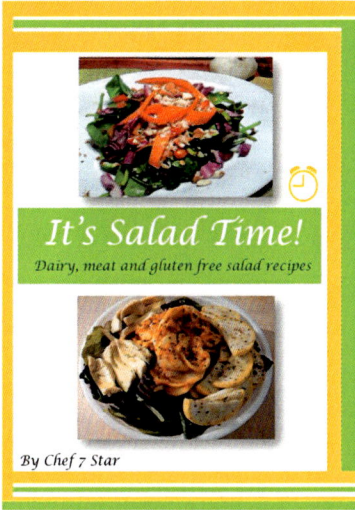

More books from Chef 7

7 steps to eat more living foods

Love-n-life

Salad time

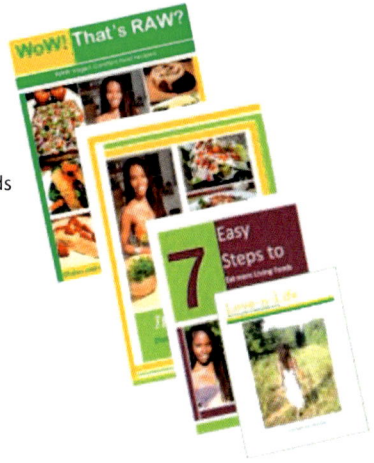

To order more books, catering or instruction contact us @ 336 273 7406

Email: illum7ination@yahoo.com …Editing by Arts E. Hinson

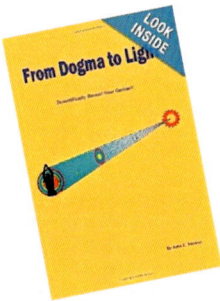

Raw Vegan foods resource

https://www.sunfired.com/

www.rawtopianbliss.org/

http://www.kheprasrawfoodjuicebar.com/

http://www.yourlifeit.com/

http://www.livingsuperfood.com/

Book by My husband Artis Hinson

"Scientifically Reveal your God Self"

FROM DOGMA TO LIGHT